8 Words

To Achieve Anything You Desire

8
Words

To Achieve Anything You Desire

Michael Hayes
Alicia Hayes
2016

Copyright © 2016 by Michael and Alicia Hayes

All rights reserved. No part of this book may be reproduced, copied, stored, or transmitted in any form or by any means – graphic, electronic, or mechanical, including photocopying, recording, or information storage and retrieval systems – without the prior written permission of the author, except where permitted by law.

The information contained in this book is intended to be educational and not for diagnosis, prescription, or treatment of any health disorders or as a substitute for financial planning. This information should not replace consultation with a competent healthcare or financial professional. The content of this book is intended to be used as an adjunct to a rational and responsible program prescribed by a healthcare practitioner or financial professional. The author and publisher are in no way liable for any misuse of the material.

First edition 2016

For information about special discounts for bulk purchase, please contact the author.

Michael and Alicia Hayes
P.O. Box 520443
Salt Lake City, Utah, 84152-0443

Email: 8wordsbook@gmail.com

www.8wordsbook.com

Manufactured in the United States of America

ISBN-13: 978-0-9979698-1-8

ISBN-10: 0-9979698-1-4

For those who are striving to improve their lives and the lives of others around them on a daily basis.

"We are what we think. All that we are arises with our thoughts. With our thoughts, we make the world."
~ BUDDHA

Contents

Chapter 1 ~ MONEY

Ace the Interview ~ 11

Get the Raise ~ 13

Get the Promotion ~ 15

Closing the Deal ~ 17

Eliminate Debt ~ 19

Successful Investments ~ 21

Winner's Luck ~ 23

Accumulate Wealth ~ 25

Chapter 2 ~ HEALTH

Power the Workout ~ 31

Diet Domination ~ 33

Power the Run ~ 35

Strengthen the Immune System ~ 37

Power Cycling ~ 39

Increase Fertility for Women ~ 41

Increase Virility for Men ~ 43

Forever Young ~ 45

Chapter 3 ~ FAMILY

Forgive Family ~ 51

Patience with Children ~ 53

Patience with Spouse ~ 55

Gratitude for Family ~ 57

Patience with Parents ~ 59

Patience with Siblings ~ 61

Patience with In-Laws ~ 63

Gain Wisdom ~ 65

Chapter 4 ~ SOCIAL

Attract Friends ~ 71

Become Outgoing ~ 73

Attract Women ~ 75

Attract Men ~ 77

Get Along ~ 79

Become Charismatic ~ 81

Become a Leader ~ 83

Making Up ~ 85

Chapter 5 ~ COURAGE

No Regrets ~ 91

Live in the Now ~ 93

Beat the Illness ~ 95

Going to Battle ~ 97

No Fear of Flight ~ 99

Before Public Speaking ~ 101

Live Full Throttle ~ 103

Before the Operation ~ 105

Chapter 6 ~ ACHIEVEMENT

Pass Any Test ~ 111

Learn the Skill ~ 113

Win the Debate ~ 115

Graduate ~ 117

Business Success ~ 119

Be Focused ~ 121

Determination ~ 123

Win at Anything ~ 125

Chapter 7 ~ MIND

Start the Day ~ 131

Open Your Mind ~ 133

Be Positive ~ 135

One of a Kind ~ 137

More Intelligent ~ 139

I'm Attractive ~ 141

I'm Creative ~ 143

I'm Lucky ~ 145

Chapter 8 ~ RECOVERY

Grief Recovery ~ 151

Addiction Recovery ~ 153

Abuse Recovery ~ 155

Job Loss Recovery ~ 157

Moving On ~ 159

Divorce Recovery ~ 161

Illness Recovery ~ 163

Financial Recovery ~ 165

My will and Divine will are One.

I am connected to the abundant flow of the Universe and easily manifest my dreams.

~ Solar Plexus Chakra ~

Introduction

This book is for anyone seeking to put their thoughts and mind in the right place at the right time and to achieve their desires, whatever they may be. Are you desiring more money? Are you desiring better health? Do you wish to overcome an addiction or a fear? Try this simple method to put your mindset in the right place so that the Universe will powerfully manifest your desires for you.

This book is intended for anyone of any belief structure, religious, agnostic or atheist. Through a combination of scientifically proven psychology and powerful ancient numerical mysticism, this book will give you a method rooted in the best of both worlds.

The First Element – The Number 8

The power of the number 8 is well known in far Eastern culture. It is an undeniably important and powerful number to millions of people on the planet earth and many people in Western culture are just beginning to recognize its significance and power.

The people who are currently familiar with the power of the number 8, use it in their lives in many untold ways. It can be found in everything from their selected phone numbers, passwords, lock combinations or even the asking price of a property or car they have for sale. The fact is, wherever and whenever they have a choice of numbers, they will make certain the number 8 is present if possible. As one historic example, when China hosted the world at the Beijing Olympics in 2008, the opening ceremony officially began at 8:00 PM China Standard Time on August 8, 2008 or 08-08-08.

As another example, in Jewish thought, the number 8 is also very significant. The number seven represents the physical world which can be touched and sensed, as in "God created the Earth in 7 days". On the other hand, the number 8 represents that which exists beyond the physical world and transcends to the metaphysical. It represents that which cannot be seen, but is present and powerful. The number 8 represents that which stirs us from within.

Simply put, 8 is a number that many people use as a focal point for success in their lives. It is backed by centuries of use by people who lived before us.

The Second Element - The Words

It is indisputable that you become what your thoughts are. You are what you think. Words become thoughts and thoughts become reality. New research studies are confirming this truth again and again. Mindset matters!

For example, in a 2014 study, researchers from Yale University and University of California, Berkeley, set out to find out just how powerful negative –- or positive – stereotypes or perceptions of aging can be. The study, published in the journal, *Psychological Science*, found implicit exposure to positive words and associations with aging were shown to be more effective on physical abilities than a similar study which prescribed six months of only exercise.

Your thoughts will manifest into reality if they are a constant presence in your life and you really believe them. It is true that your thoughts affect who you are. A negative person tends to attract negativity into his or her life. In contrast, a positive person attracts positivity. This is simple common sense, right? Yes. However, our lives are very complicated and busy. Each of us experiences many different challenges in life that can either make this "common sense" of positive versus negative, easy to follow or extremely difficult.

The purpose of "8 Words" is to give you a simple tool to use during those difficult times in your life, to focus your thoughts in an effective and positive way, in a direction that will manifest what you want and need at any given time. Use this book and its various chapters to put your mind in the right mode to over-power and defeat negativity and allow the Universe to flow in your direction, giving you the positive results which you desire.

This book combines two very powerful tools; the ancient power of the number 8 and the time tested "you are what you think" truism. Follow the suggested instructions within any chapter you choose to utilize, to focus your mind and thoughts for that desire which you have selected. When you see how this book works for you, share it with a friend or family member who needs help achieving their desires. May the overwhelming power of your mind, the Universe and your thoughts, bring you great success going forward.

Using Your 8 Words

Select a chapter that pertains to your desires. In a private place, preferably where you are alone, say the 8 words listed to yourself one by one, while placing your forefinger or thumb upon the number 8 at the bottom of the page. Doing this will connect your thoughts to the strength of the number 8.

Start with the first listed word and think deeply of that word and its meaning every time you say it to yourself. Think of the meaning of each word in the context of what you are trying to achieve. Move through the list methodically word by word until you have said all 8 words in the list to yourself. After you have done a "set" of 8 words, repeat the process as often as you wish. You will notice that certain words in the list of 8 will resonate with you and speak to you for this situation. Choose one or more of these words which speak to you or feel right and continue to think of them throughout your day or during the critical times which you need them.

When is it best to do a set of 8 Words? For a meeting or an event, do your words just prior or as close as possible in time. Perhaps in your car upon arrival at the meeting or event. Perhaps just before leaving for the meeting or event. For a desired lifestyle or general mindset, use your words daily at the same time or multiple times throughout the day. Intuitively, you will know which technique for use is best for you for any particular list of 8 words you are focusing on. Each chapter in this book will have an introduction which repeats these instructions.

"Some people want it to happen, some wish it would happen, others make it happen."
~ Michael Jordan
(professional basketball player and business man)

CHAPTER ONE

MONEY

Ace the Interview ~ 11

Get the Raise ~ 13

Get the Promotion ~ 15

Closing the Deal ~ 17

Eliminate Debt ~ 19

Successful Investments ~ 21

Winner's Luck ~ 23

Accumulate Wealth ~ 25

Instructions

In a private place, preferably where you are alone, say the 8 words listed to yourself, one by one, while placing your forefinger or thumb upon the number 8 which is present on the page. Doing this will connect your thoughts to the strength of the number 8.

Start with the first listed word and think deeply of that word and its meaning every time you say it to yourself. Think of the meaning of each word in the context of what you are trying to achieve. Move through the list methodically word by word until you have said all 8 words in the list to yourself. After you have done a "set" of 8 words, repeat the process as often as you wish, if time permits. You will notice that certain words in the list of 8 will resonate with you and "speak" to you for this situation. Choose one or more of these words which "speak" to you or "feel right" and continue to think of them throughout your day or during the critical times which you need them.

Ace the Interview

"I say these 8 words one at a time, while touching the number, in true belief as my own thoughts, to achieve my desires."

Confident

Tenacious

Skilled

Knowledgeable

Destined

Equipped

Brave

Doubtless

Get the Raise

"I say these 8 words one at a time, while touching the number, in true belief as my own thoughts, to achieve my desires."

Deserved

Time

Higher

Payoff

Owed

Valuable

Proven

Destined

Get the Promotion

"I say these 8 words one at a time, while touching the number, in true belief as my own thoughts, to achieve my desires."

Best

Strong

Knowledgeable

Expert

Direction

Deserving

Proven

Destined

Closing the Deal

"I say these 8 words one at a time, while touching the number, in true belief as my own thoughts, to achieve my desires."

Intelligent

Knowledge

Focused

Rapport

Empathize

Overcome

Solve

Agreement

Eliminate Debt

"I say these 8 words one at a time, while touching the number, in true belief as my own thoughts, to achieve my desires."

Control

Tenacity

Motivation

Secure

Freedom

Build

Fortune

Power

Successful Investments

"I say these 8 words one at a time, while touching the number, in true belief as my own thoughts, to achieve my desires."

Foresight

Timely

Intuition

Knowledge

Opportunity

Savvy

Value

Act

Winner's Luck

"I say these 8 words one at a time, while touching the number, in true belief as my own thoughts, to achieve my desires."

Destined

Lucky

Me

Timing

Feeling

Channel

Happen

Will

Accumulate Wealth

"I say these 8 words one at a time, while touching the number, in true belief as my own thoughts, to achieve my desires."

Universe

Destined

Savvy

Power

Gratitude

Control

Positive

Attraction

"Step out of the history that is holding you back. Step into the new story you are willing to create."
~ Oprah Winfrey
(talk show host, actress, producer and philanthropist)

CHAPTER TWO

HEALTH

Power the Workout ~ 31

Diet Domination ~ 33

Power the Run ~ 35

Strengthen the Immune System ~ 37

Power Cycling ~ 39

Increase Fertility for Women ~ 41

Increase Virility for Men ~ 43

Forever Young ~ 45

Instructions

In a private place, preferably where you are alone, say the 8 words listed to yourself, one by one, while placing your forefinger or thumb upon the number 8 which is present on the page. Doing this will connect your thoughts to the strength of the number 8.

Start with the first listed word and think deeply of that word and its meaning every time you say it to yourself. Think of the meaning of each word in the context of what you are trying to achieve. Move through the list methodically word by word until you have said all 8 words in the list to yourself. After you have done a "set" of 8 words, repeat the process as often as you wish, if time permits. You will notice that certain words in the list of 8 will resonate with you and "speak" to you for this situation. Choose one or more of these words which "speak" to you or "feel right" and continue to think of them throughout your day or during the critical times which you need them.

Power the Workout

"I say these 8 words one at a time, while touching the number, in true belief as my own thoughts, to achieve my desires."

Powerful

Strong

Tenacity

Push

Accelerate

Breathe

Focus

Repetition

Diet Domination

"I say these 8 words one at a time, while touching the number, in true belief as my own thoughts, to achieve my desires."

Me

Obedience

Will

Time

Persistent

Destined

Focused

Life

Power the Run

"I say these 8 words one at a time, while touching the number, in true belief as my own thoughts, to achieve my desires."

Stamina

Freedom

Power

Independence

Focused

Me

Vitality

Meditate

Strengthen the Immune System

"I say these 8 words one at a time, while touching the number, in true belief as my own thoughts, to achieve my desires."

Cleanse

Detoxify

Workout

Nutrients

Strength

Positive

Energy

Hydrate

Power Cycling

"I say these 8 words one at a time, while touching the number, in true belief as my own thoughts, to achieve my desires."

Challenge

Intensity

Accelerate

Muscle

Power

Distance

Zone

Leader

Increase Fertility for Women

"I say these 8 words one at a time, while touching the number, in true belief as my own thoughts, to achieve my desires."

Feminine

Healthy

Nurture

Ready

Passionate

Devoted

Strong

Believe

Increase Virility for Men

"I say these 8 words one at a time, while touching the number, in true belief as my own thoughts, to achieve my desires."

Potency

Hunt

Seduce

Lust

Energize

Tenacious

Pleasure

Female

Forever Young

"I say these 8 words one at a time, while touching the number, in true belief as my own thoughts, to achieve my desires."

Passion

Funny

Positive

Humor

Healthy

Fearless

Opportunity

Timeless

"You have to work hard to get your thinking clean to make it simple. But it's worth it in the end because once you get there, you can move mountains."
~ Steve Jobs
(information technology entrepreneur and inventor)

CHAPTER THREE

FAMILY

Forgive Family ~ 51

Patience with Children ~ 53

Patience with Spouse ~ 55

Gratitude for Family ~ 57

Patience with Parents ~ 59

Patience with Siblings ~ 61

Patience with In-Laws ~ 63

Gain Wisdom ~ 65

Instructions

In a private place, preferably where you are alone, say the 8 words listed to yourself, one by one, while placing your forefinger or thumb upon the number 8 which is present on the page. Doing this will connect your thoughts to the strength of the number 8.

Start with the first listed word and think deeply of that word and its meaning every time you say it to yourself. Think of the meaning of each word in the context of what you are trying to achieve. Move through the list methodically word by word until you have said all 8 words in the list to yourself. After you have done a "set" of 8 words, repeat the process as often as you wish, if time permits. You will notice that certain words in the list of 8 will resonate with you and "speak" to you for this situation. Choose one or more of these words which "speak" to you or "feel right" and continue to think of them throughout your day or during the critical times which you need them.

Forgive Family

"I say these 8 words one at a time, while touching the number, in true belief as my own thoughts, to achieve my desires."

Humility

Gratitude

Recognize

Centered

Patience

Greater

Love

Truth

Patience with Children

"I say these 8 words one at a time, while touching the number, in true belief as my own thoughts, to achieve my desires."

Gratitude

Responsibility

Nurture

Teach

Guide

Humility

Selfless

Duty

Patience with Spouse

"I say these 8 words one at a time, while touching the number, in true belief as my own thoughts, to achieve my desires."

Love

Commitment

Humility

Gratitude

Journey

Forgive

Strive

Responsible

Gratitude for Family

"I say these 8 words one at a time, while touching the number, in true belief as my own thoughts, to achieve my desires."

Love

Patience

Support

Together

Caring

Team

Bond

Compromise

Patience with Parents

"I say these 8 words one at a time, while touching the number, in true belief as my own thoughts, to achieve my desires."

Respect

Value

Intelligent

Bond

Humor

Connected

Assist

Lesson

Patience with Siblings

"I say these 8 words one at a time, while touching the number, in true belief as my own thoughts, to achieve my desires."

Team

Destined

Respect

Mutual

Bond

Protective

Guardian

Love

Patience with In-laws

"I say these 8 words one at a time, while touching the number, in true belief as my own thoughts, to achieve my desires."

Acceptance

Appreciation

Reciprocal

Bond

Respect

Spouse

Inevitable

Destiny

Gain Wisdom

"I say these 8 words one at a time, while touching the number, in true belief as my own thoughts, to achieve my desires."

Calm

Methodical

Reasoned

Maturity

Sensible

Humility

Realistic

Purposeful

"When you dance, your purpose is not to get to a certain place on the floor. It's to enjoy each step along the way."
~ Dr. Wayne Dyer
(philosopher, author and motivational speaker)

CHAPTER FOUR

SOCIAL

Attract Friends ~ 71

Become Outgoing ~ 73

Attract Women ~ 75

Attract Men ~ 77

Get Along ~ 79

Become Charismatic ~ 81

Become a Leader ~ 83

Making Up ~ 85

Instructions

In a private place, preferably where you are alone, say the 8 words listed to yourself, one by one, while placing your forefinger or thumb upon the number 8 which is present on the page. Doing this will connect your thoughts to the strength of the number 8.

Start with the first listed word and think deeply of that word and its meaning every time you say it to yourself. Think of the meaning of each word in the context of what you are trying to achieve. Move through the list methodically word by word until you have said all 8 words in the list to yourself. After you have done a "set" of 8 words, repeat the process as often as you wish, if time permits. You will notice that certain words in the list of 8 will resonate with you and "speak" to you for this situation. Choose one or more of these words which "speak" to you or "feel right" and continue to think of them throughout your day or during the critical times which you need them.

Attract Friends

"I say these 8 words one at a time, while touching the number, in true belief as my own thoughts, to achieve my desires."

Open

Yes

Positive

Confident

Commonality

Adventure

Selfless

Join

Become Outgoing

"I say these 8 words one at a time, while touching the number, in true belief as my own thoughts, to achieve my desires."

Willingness

Yes

Venture

Curious

Join

Unafraid

Selfless

Contribute

Attract Women

"I say these 8 words one at a time, while touching the number, in true belief as my own thoughts, to achieve my desires."

Responsible

Confidence

Humor

Selfless

Ambitious

Partner

Groomed

Gentle

<u>Attract Men</u>

"I say these 8 words one at a time, while touching the number, in true belief as my own thoughts, to achieve my desires."

Confident

Fashionable

Selfless

Ambitious

Flirtatious

Partner

Valuable

Nurturing

Get Along

"I say these 8 words one at a time, while touching the number, in true belief as my own thoughts, to achieve my desires."

Communicate

Appreciate

Compromise

Listen

Accept

Team

Success

Cooperation

<u>Become Charismatic</u>

"I say these 8 words one at a time, while touching the number, in true belief as my own thoughts, to achieve my desires."

Unique

Style

Original

Outgoing

Humor

Positive

Warm

Laughter

Become a Leader

"I say these 8 words one at a time, while touching the number, in true belief as my own thoughts, to achieve my desires."

Determined

Confident

Challenge

Strength

Power

Outgoing

Accomplish

Forward

Making Up

"I say these 8 words one at a time, while touching the number, in true belief as my own thoughts, to achieve my desires."

Apologize

Sincere

Caring

Accept

Forgive

Respect

Appreciate

Communicate

"Life opens up opportunities to you, and you either take them or you stay afraid of taking them."
~Jim Carrey
(actor, comedian, screenwriter and producer)

CHAPTER FIVE

COURAGE

No Regrets ~ 91

Live in the Now ~ 93

Beat the Illness ~ 95

Going to Battle ~ 97

No Fear of Flight ~ 99

Before Public Speaking ~ 101

Live Full Throttle ~ 103

Before the Operation ~ 105

Instructions

In a private place, preferably where you are alone, say the 8 words listed to yourself, one by one, while placing your forefinger or thumb upon the number 8 which is present on the page. Doing this will connect your thoughts to the strength of the number 8.

Start with the first listed word and think deeply of that word and its meaning every time you say it to yourself. Think of the meaning of each word in the context of what you are trying to achieve. Move through the list methodically word by word until you have said all 8 words in the list to yourself. After you have done a "set" of 8 words, repeat the process as often as you wish, if time permits. You will notice that certain words in the list of 8 will resonate with you and "speak" to you for this situation. Choose one or more of these words which "speak" to you or "feel right" and continue to think of them throughout your day or during the critical times which you need them.

No Regrets

"I say these 8 words one at a time, while touching the number, in true belief as my own thoughts, to achieve my desires."

Forward

Confident

Reasoned

Purpose

Closure

Accomplished

Action

Ambition

Live in the Now

"I say these 8 words one at a time, while touching the number, in true belief as my own thoughts, to achieve my desires."

Opportunity

Open

Adventure

Fearless

Gratitude

Give

Act

Explore

Beat the Illness

"I say these 8 words one at a time, while touching the number, in true belief as my own thoughts, to achieve my desires."

Temporary

Immune

Strength

Future

Will

Doubtless

Positivity

Winner

Going to Battle

"I say these 8 words one at a time, while touching the number, in true belief as my own thoughts, to achieve my desires."

Purpose

Strong

Tenacious

Team

Aware

Equipped

Selfless

Focus

No Fear of Flight

"I say these 8 words one at a time, while touching the number, in true belief as my own thoughts, to achieve my desires."

Breathe

Efficient

Relax

Support

Meditate

Positive

Smile

Adventure

Before Speaking Publicly

"I say these 8 words one at a time, while touching the number, in true belief as my own thoughts, to achieve my desires."

Smart

Calm

Purpose

Teach

Clarity

Equipped

Brevity

Humorous

<u>Live Full Throttle</u>

"I say these 8 words one at a time, while touching the number, in true belief as my own thoughts, to achieve my desires."

Now

Vitality

Everything

Curious

Take

Give

Action

Reach

Before the Operation

"I say these 8 words one at a time, while touching the number, in true belief as my own thoughts, to achieve my desires."

Professionalism

Proven

Purpose

Calm

Forward

Improve

Future

Winner

"The ladder of success is best climbed my stepping on the rungs of opportunity."
~ Ayn Rand
(novelist, philosopher and screenwriter)

CHAPTER SIX

ACHIEVEMENT

Pass Any Test ~ 111

Learn the Skill ~ 113

Win the Debate ~ 115

Graduate ~ 117

Business Success ~ 119

Be Focused ~ 121

Determination ~ 123

Win at Anything ~ 125

Instructions

In a private place, preferably where you are alone, say the 8 words listed to yourself, one by one, while placing your forefinger or thumb upon the number 8 which is present on the page. Doing this will connect your thoughts to the strength of the number 8.

Start with the first listed word and think deeply of that word and its meaning every time you say it to yourself. Think of the meaning of each word in the context of what you are trying to achieve. Move through the list methodically word by word until you have said all 8 words in the list to yourself. After you have done a "set" of 8 words, repeat the process as often as you wish, if time permits. You will notice that certain words in the list of 8 will resonate with you and "speak" to you for this situation. Choose one or more of these words which "speak" to you or "feel right" and continue to think of them throughout your day or during the critical times which you need them.

Pass Any Test

"I say these 8 words one at a time, while touching the number, in true belief as my own thoughts, to achieve my desires."

Confident

Achieve

Prepared

Success

Determined

Goal

Forward

Proud

Learn the Skill

"I say these 8 words one at a time, while touching the number, in true belief as my own thoughts, to achieve my desires."

Focus

Study

Curious

Dedication

Driven

Technical

Strive

Respect

Win the Debate

"I say these 8 words one at a time, while touching the number, in true belief as my own thoughts, to achieve my desires."

Prepared

Logic

Doubtless

Educated

Tenacious

Strategic

Exploit

Right

<u>Graduate</u>

"I say these 8 words one at a time, while touching the number, in true belief as my own thoughts, to achieve my desires."

Dedicated

Tenacious

Fortitude

Driven

Fearless

Prepared

Destiny

Success

Business Success

"I say these 8 words one at a time, while touching the number, in true belief as my own thoughts, to achieve my desires."

Belief

Knowledge

Unique

Service

Creative

Inventive

Innovative

Mine

<u>Be Focused</u>

"I say these 8 words one at a time, while touching the number, in true belief as my own thoughts, to achieve my desires."

Singular

Narrow

One

Smart

Vision

Sense

Goal

Successful

<u>Determination</u>

"I say these 8 words one at a time, while touching the number, in true belief as my own thoughts, to achieve my desires."

Focus

Strength

Unsatisfied

Hungry

Tenacious

Grip

Stubborn

Will

Win at Anything

"I say these 8 words one at a time, while touching the number, in true belief as my own thoughts, to achieve my desires."

Knowledge

Prepared

Creative

Tenacious

Driven

Smart

Focused

Destiny

"There are two ways to live: You can live as if nothing is a miracle; you can live as if everything is a miracle."
~ Albert Einstein
(physicist and scientist)

CHAPTER SEVEN

MIND

Start the Day ~ 131

Open Your Mind ~ 133

Be Positive ~ 135

One of a Kind ~ 137

More Intelligent ~ 139

I'm Attractive ~ 141

I'm Creative ~ 143

I'm Lucky ~ 145

Instructions

In a private place, preferably where you are alone, say the 8 words listed to yourself, one by one, while placing your forefinger or thumb upon the number 8 which is present on the page. Doing this will connect your thoughts to the strength of the number 8.

Start with the first listed word and think deeply of that word and its meaning every time you say it to yourself. Think of the meaning of each word in the context of what you are trying to achieve. Move through the list methodically word by word until you have said all 8 words in the list to yourself. After you have done a "set" of 8 words, repeat the process as often as you wish, if time permits. You will notice that certain words in the list of 8 will resonate with you and "speak" to you for this situation. Choose one or more of these words which "speak" to you or "feel right" and continue to think of them throughout your day or during the critical times which you need them.

Start the Day

"I say these 8 words one at a time, while touching the number, in true belief as my own thoughts, to achieve my desires."

Gratitude

Positive

Blessings

Determination

Meditate

Focus

Organized

Smile

Open Your Mind

"I say these 8 words one at a time, while touching the number, in true belief as my own thoughts, to achieve my desires."

Yes

Opportunity

New

Adventure

Change

Now

Positive

Open

<u>Be Positive</u>

"I say these 8 words one at a time, while touching the number, in true belief as my own thoughts, to achieve my desires."

Gratitude

Accomplish

Fulfilled

Beauty

Learning

Adventure

Outlook

Believe

One of a Kind

"I say these 8 words one at a time, while touching the number, in true belief as my own thoughts, to achieve my desires."

Unique

Wonderful

Special

Loved

Independent

Original

Amazing

Leader

More Intelligent

"I say these 8 words one at a time, while touching the number, in true belief as my own thoughts, to achieve my desires."

Confident

Brave

Challenge

Power

Determination

Success

Control

Understand

I'm Attractive

"I say these 8 words one at a time, while touching the number, in true belief as my own thoughts, to achieve my desires."

Style

Confident

Outgoing

Posture

Smile

Pride

Unique

Fresh

I'm Creative

"I say these 8 words one at a time, while touching the number, in true belief as my own thoughts, to achieve my desires."

Possibility

Soul

Endless

Imagination

Adventure

Challenge

Colorful

Embrace

I'm Lucky

"I say these 8 words one at a time, while touching the number, in true belief as my own thoughts, to achieve my desires."

Fortunate

Successful

Positive

Blessed

Promising

Favored

Opportunity

Timing

"You may not control all the events that happen to you, but you can decide not to be reduced by them."
~ Maya Angelou
(poet, memoirist and civil rights activist)

CHAPTER EIGHT

RECOVERY

Grief Recovery ~ 151

Addiction Recovery ~ 153

Abuse Recovery ~ 155

Job Loss Recovery ~ 157

Moving On ~ 159

Divorce Recovery ~ 161

Illness Recovery ~ 163

Financial Recovery ~ 165

Instructions

In a private place, preferably where you are alone, say the 8 words listed to yourself, one by one, while placing your forefinger or thumb upon the number 8 which is present on the page. Doing this will connect your thoughts to the strength of the number 8.

Start with the first listed word and think deeply of that word and its meaning every time you say it to yourself. Think of the meaning of each word in the context of what you are trying to achieve. Move through the list methodically word by word until you have said all 8 words in the list to yourself. After you have done a "set" of 8 words, repeat the process as often as you wish, if time permits. You will notice that certain words in the list of 8 will resonate with you and "speak" to you for this situation. Choose one or more of these words which "speak" to you or "feel right" and continue to think of them throughout your day or during the critical times which you need them.

Grief Recovery

"I say these 8 words one at a time, while touching the number, in true belief as my own thoughts, to achieve my desires."

Gratitude

Honor

Survive

Forward

Release

Comfort

Breathe

Peace

<u>Addiction Recovery</u>

"I say these 8 words one at a time, while touching the number, in true belief as my own thoughts, to achieve my desires."

Done

Future

Smart

Self

Dedicated

Health

Positive

Life

Abuse Recovery

"I say these 8 words one at a time, while touching the number, in true belief as my own thoughts, to achieve my desires."

Better

Dignity

Done

Forward

Strong

Friends

Love

Life

Job Loss Recovery

"I say these 8 words one at a time, while touching the number, in true belief as my own thoughts, to achieve my desires."

Valuable

Knowledge

Attractive

Needed

Skillful

Player

Destined

Winner

Moving On

"I say these 8 words one at a time, while touching the number, in true belief as my own thoughts, to achieve my desires."

Learn

Empower

Strong

Independent

Self

Improve

Sufficient

Brave

Divorce Recovery

"I say these 8 words one at a time, while touching the number, in true belief as my own thoughts, to achieve my desires."

Forward

Confident

Social

Purpose

Gratitude

Improvement

Release

Turn

Illness Recovery

"I say these 8 words one at a time, while touching the number, in true belief as my own thoughts, to achieve my desires."

Determine

Positive

Strong

Will

Love

Support

Family

Friends

Financial Recovery

"I say these 8 words one at a time, while touching the number, in true belief as my own thoughts, to achieve my desires."

Secure

Power

Discipline

Budget

Freedom

Balance

Proud

Life

Words Matter…

Suggest words for our 2nd edition.

We want your input for the words that will appear in the second edition of *8 Words To Achieve Anything You Desire*.

Feel free to make your suggestions and
we will select "consensus" words from these responses.

Website: www.8wordsbook.com
Facebook: www.facebook.com/8wordsbook
Email: 8wordsbook@gmail.com

www.ingramcontent.com/pod-product-compliance
Lightning Source LLC
Chambersburg PA
CBHW020615300426
44113CB00007B/656